THE SECRET POWER
OF THE PYRAMIDS

THE SECRET POWER OF THE PYRAMIDS

BY W.R. AKINS

Franklin Watts
New York/London/Toronto/Sydney/1980

Frontispiece: pyramids in Giza, Egypt.

Diagrams by Vantage Art, Inc.
Design by Paul Perlow

Photographs courtesy of: Wide World Photos: frontispiece, pp. 13, 17, 18, 19, 20, 43, 44; United Press International: pp. 5, 14, 24; Culver Pictures: pp. 6, 32.

Library of Congress Cataloging in Publication Data

Akins, W   R
The secret power of the pyramids.

Bibliography: p.
Includes index.
SUMMARY: Discusses the mysterious origins of the Egyptian pyramids and the strange power that the pyramid structure has had over people's imaginations throughout the ages. Also explores the hypothesis that the pyramids are clues to an ancient advanced science.
1. Pyramids—Egypt—Miscellanea—Juvenile literature.
2. Pyramids—Miscellanea—Juvenile literature. 3. Occult sciences—Juvenile literature.
[1. Pyramids—Egypt. 2. Pyramids. 3. Occult sciences]
I. Title.
BF1999.A57   001.9   79-24972
ISBN 0-531-02929-8

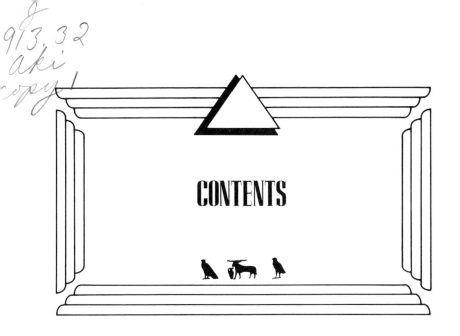

CONTENTS

FOR MARY
when she grows up

THE SECRET POWER
OF THE PYRAMIDS

PREFACE

Were the Egyptian pyramids built at the command of the ancient pharaohs, or were they built by extraterrestrial visitors?

Did Napoleon really read his future downfall in the king's chamber of the Great Pyramid at Giza?

Do the pyramids contain a message left by the gods? Are they the storehouse of the earth's past and future history?

Can plastic or cardboard models of the pyramids make plants grow faster, preserve food, sharpen razor blades, and help to heal and control pain?

Is there such a thing as "pyramid power," and can it be acquired by any one of us?

I don't know, at least not for sure. There is probably some truth in the claims of those who believe in pyramidology, and there is probably some truth in what their critics say. I can only judge on the basis of my own experience and hope that you will do the same.

One fact is certain. The pyramids have always held a strange power over people's imaginations. For centuries we have wondered at their size and engineering, their history, and the tales of their mystery and secret power. New facts, new studies, and new discoveries by scientists have destroyed many of our old ideas about the pyramids but in doing so, they have added to their mystery.

"Scientists recently conducted a computer study of the Cheops pyramid," said Dr. Gunther Rosenberg, founder and former president of the European Occult Research Society. Dr. Rosenberg is a pyramidologist who has devoted his life to solving the mysteries behind these primitive stone creations. "The experts walked away shaking their heads in disbelief! At present, we don't know who built the pyramids, why they were built, or the reasons for their existence.

"However, new data has proven that the pyramids may be a clue to an ancient, advanced science," continued Dr. Rosenberg. "This tremendously advanced science ruled the world many thousands of years before Christ was born. The builders of the pyramids knew many secrets of the universe. They understood advanced mathematics. Their knowledge of world geography was amazing. Some of the data built into the pyramid is just now being proven by our space scientists. Ultimately, we will have to revise our textbooks and rewrite the history of mankind."

Is Dr. Rosenberg right? Many other scientists say that pyramidology is "sheer bunk," and that there is no such thing as pyramid power. They consider the subject as occult, or a study of the supernatural. Are they right? I shall try to explain this controversial and ever-expanding interest in pyramidology. I will describe some of my own experiments with pyramid power, both when they worked and when they failed, and I will tell you of some tests you can perform yourself.

Whether or not pyramid power works for you, you will enjoy testing it out. Above everything else, you should share this book with a friend because both of you will want to compare the results of your experiments with pyramid power.

THE
MYSTERIES OF THE PYRAMIDS

In 1968, Dr. Luis Alvarez, who won the Nobel prize in physics that year, set out to determine scientifically whether there were any secret chambers or passages in Chephren's pyramid at Giza. To solve the mystery, Dr. Alvarez decided to use a new method of scientific measurement. He measured the bombardment of cosmic rays passing through the pyramid. A cosmic particle recording device would show a greater drop in energy when the rays passed through a hidden chamber than it would when they passed through solid stone. Scientists from different institutions and different nations participated in the experiment which was carried out with the endorsement of both the United States and Egypt.

After measuring over two million rays, magnetic tapes were used to record the data. The most modern computers were used to analyze the results. John Tunstall, a reporter for *The Times* of London, quoted one of the scientists in charge of the project as saying, "It defies all known laws of physics." The tapes revealed that the patterns of the cosmic particles could not be measured. Worse yet, every time the tapes were re-run on the computers, the patterns were different. In addition, not only were the cosmic particles rearranged, but certain data disappeared from the tapes.

"This is scientifically impossible," said one of the scientists, Dr. Amr Goneid, to John Tunstall.

The Times' reporter then asked, "Has all the scientific know-how been rendered useless by some force beyond man's comprehension?"

Dr. Goneid answered: "Either the geometry of the pyramid is in substantial error, which would affect our readings, or there is a mystery which is beyond our understanding—call it what you will, occultism, the curse of the pharaohs, sorcery, or magic; there is some force which defies the laws of science at work in the pyramid."

Certainly, there are mysteries of the pyramids, especially the Great Pyramid of Giza, beyond our understanding. But do we have to assume that there is some force operating which "defies the laws of science?" Although Dr. Rosenberg may well prove to be right, let us begin by reviewing some concrete facts about this wonder of wonders—the Great Pyramid of the Pharaoh Cheops. In this way, we shall arrive at our first mystery.

The Great Pyramid is massive. If you picture in your mind a 40-story building rising from a 13.1-acre (5.3-hectares) base, you will get a good idea of the size of the pyramid. The base of the structure would cover almost one-fifth of a square mile of downtown London or New York or Chicago. It is estimated that it contains over two and a half million limestone building blocks. These blocks weigh from 3 to 15 tons each (2.7 to 13.6 metric tons). When Napoleon marched

**Camel riders are dwarfed
by the Great Pyramid of the
Pharaoh Cheops at Giza.**

his army through Egypt, he estimated that there was enough stone in the Great Pyramid to build a wall around France, a wall ten feet (3.0 m) high and a foot (.3 m) thick. Actually, the Emperor of France underestimated the size of the Great Pyramid. If we were to grind the stone in this huge structure into gravel, we could lay a road 18 feet (5.5 m) wide and a foot (.3 m) thick from New York to Salt Lake City or from London to Moscow. If we cut all the building blocks into one-foot cubes (196.6 cc), we could build a stone chain two-thirds of the way around the world at its equator.

Stone for stone, the Great Pyramid is large enough to contain all the major cathedrals of Rome, Florence, and Milan. And you would still have room left to include the Empire State Building, Westminster Abbey, St. Paul's Cathedral in London, and the British Houses of Parliament. In fact, there is more stone in the Great Pyramid than was used to build every church in England since the birth of Christ. And every building block is hewn with the precision of a jeweler cutting diamonds.

These huge limestone casings were cut, dressed, and fitted together so well that a business card cannot be inserted between the joints. The cement used is so fine and yet so strong that the tons of limestone blocks will fracture before the cement gives, although less than a fiftieth of an inch (.1 cm) separates the blocks.

More remarkable is the engineering required to build this 6½-million-ton (5.85 million metric tons) structure. How

**The size of each limestone used
to build this small section of
the Pyramid of Cheops, makes it
difficult to imagine how humans
hauled such huge stones into place.**

could such massive stones have been transported to the building site? How could such huge stones have been hauled into place? Why is there such a difference between the workmanship of the Great Pyramid and that of a nearby pyramid built only one generation earlier? Some of the stones are fitted with seamless joints. The masons who dressed these stones were able to estimate that 2,000 tons (1,800 metric tons) of pressure per square inch (6.45 sq cm) would be required. How was the ancient Egyptian worker able to apply such pressure with such primitive tools as an axe made from copper strapped to a piece of wood with leather thongs and levels and squares hewn from wood?

More mysterious than the construction of the Great Pyramid is the mathematical knowledge which went into its building. For example, imagine a map of the world. If you drew a line from the North Pole to the South Pole so that it crossed the greatest possible body of water, where would you draw it? Of course, over the Pacific Ocean. On the other hand, if you were to draw a similar line crossing the greatest amount of land, the line would run roughly through Finland, Turkey, and Egypt to Cape Town, South Africa. The Great Pyramid is situated within minutes of the middle of that line. The pyramid is also oriented precisely to the four points of the compass.

The siting of the Great Pyramid is remarkable, but its measurements are even more remarkable. So rigorous is the geometry of the Great Pyramid that if you double its height and divide that into its perimeter, you would have a close approximation of the mathematical ratio *pi*. According to historians, the theory of *pi* was not known until Pythagoras discovered it—almost two thousand years after the Great Pyramid was built. Egyptian weights and measures have continued to baffle us. The ancient Egyptians used a variety of cubits, spans, palms, and digits which obey no single standard which we know. Probably the closest estimate of Egyptian measurements is that formed by Charles Piazzi Smyth. He calculated that the "pyramid inch" corresponds to 1.001 of the modern inch (2.543 cm.).

According to pyramidologists, the construction of the Great Pyramid required a more sophisticated knowledge of astronomy, geometry and other disciplines then ancient people could possibly have had. They also believe that the measurements of the pyramid are a secret code which reveals the future of civilization. These prophecies foretell the events of the Old Testament and the future up to and including the Second Coming of Christ.

So advanced is the store of knowledge used to build the Great Pyramid of Cheops that many pyramidologists believe it was not built by the Egyptians at all. They maintain that it was built by the people who fled from the lost continent of Atlantis—or by extraterrestrial beings. Sounds far-fetched, doesn't it? Fortunately for those of us who are skeptical, there is a way out of the problem.

If the pyramidologists are wrong, all we have to do is throw out all our old ideas about what our ancestors knew and did not know. We just have to admit that primitive people were a great deal more sophisticated than we gave them credit for, perhaps more sophisticated than we are today. Most people don't like to change their ideas. They would rather cling to the notion that early people were primitive and that we are civilized. Anyway, we would have to rewrite all our history books.

On the other hand, if the pyramidologists are right— what then?

THE GREAT PYRAMID
AND THE OCCULT DOCTRINE

Why were the pyramids built? Most people think of the pyramids as the tombs of the ancient kings and queens of Egypt—their additional function as temples is largely ignored. Yet the very structure of the Great Pyramid expresses certain religious beliefs and magical rites of the ancient Egyptians.

According to what we presently understand regarding Heliopolitan beliefs, when the pharaoh ceased his earthly life, he went to rejoin the sun gods. According to other scholars, the pharaoh was identified with the sun gods, his earthly life an incarnation of one of them. For this reason, the pyramid was regarded not merely as the pharaoh's tomb but also as a symbol of his ascension. The steps of the pyramid were referred to as a stairway or ladder leading to the heavens. Some scholars have even thought that the edges of the pyramid and its steeply inclined passageways represent the rays of the sun as they tear apart the clouds and descend to earth.

Although the building of the pyramids probably derives from the prehistoric mound (tomb) cultures, the influence of Mesopotamian thought on early Egyptian culture may have dictated their use as temples as well. Throughout the Middle

East, the prevailing religious beliefs required the erection of tall structures to bring devotees close to their sun gods. For example, in Mesopotamia tall brick towers called *ziggurats* were built for this purpose. There are scholars who believe that the Tower of Babel was actually a Babylonian *ziggurat*.

Prior to the burial mound cultures, people disposed of the dead by leaving them on mountain tops and other high places. There they would be consumed by animals, birds, and the elements. We do not know what caused the transition to the burial mound. In any event, the pyramid, which resembles a mountain, partakes of its symbolism. This symbolism is explained by Professor G. Posener, in his book *Dictionary of Egyptian Civilization:* "It is not difficult to imagine that the mound, although purely practical in origin, was thought to resemble the hill which had emerged from the primeval waters when the earth came into being and thus represented existence. Death could be magically countered by the presence of this potent symbol."

ANCIENT EGYPTIAN
RELIGIOUS BELIEFS

However, these sophisticated ideas of an after-life did not develop all at once. Originally, animals were sacred to the Egyptians. The earliest tribes, in the days before the pharaohs,

Ziggurats, towers built by the early Babylonians and Assyrians, are believed to have been used to bring devotees close to their sun gods. This one, dating from about 1580, is probably the tallest one still standing in Iraq.

venerated their own gods, and each was identified with a particular animal, such as the cat at Bubastis and the bull Apis at Memphis.

As Egyptian civilization advanced, the gods became humanized. Some had human bodies but retained the heads of animals. The common belief was that the earth was a disk with Egypt as its midpoint, and that the surrounding mountains supported it—above what? The notion was that without that support the world would sink into the abysmal waters of the underworld.

From a small handful of new gods, half-human, half-animal, such as Osiris, Isis, and Horus, there emerged the awesome figure of Ra, the Sun God, whose symbol was the pyramid. By the nineteenth dynasty, Ra was combined with the other most prominent Egyptian deity, Amon, to be known as the almighty Amon-Ra, Lord of the Worlds. To worship these gods, the average person was dependent on the priesthood. The reigning pharaoh was the channel of divine wisdom. He and the priests, by long and arduous training in the spiritual disciplines, became worthy of initiation into the secrets of the cosmos and were venerated during their lives and worshipped after their deaths.

As we learn from the *Egyptian Book of the Dead,* the deceased was provided with food and drink, weapons, toilet articles, and even a funerary boat by which to make his or her way to the shores of the land of spirits. This provision of

This chamber, found 200 feet (60 m) in a mountain on the Nile, contains four seated figures representing the gods Ptah, Amon-Ra, Re-Horakhte and Rameses II.

(15)

food, tools, and so forth, was not as childish as it might at first appear. The Egyptians did not expect the dead to make actual use of these articles.

It was believed that every person had at least two bodies: a physical body and an exact spiritual duplicate. All material objects were supposed to have spiritual counterparts. It was believed that the spirit of the dead would be able to make use of the spiritual counterparts of the objects provided.

This belief may also underlie the process of mummification. As long as the physical body was preserved, the spirit would be able to move about in the after-life. Mummification may also have been used to prevent reincarnation, but it seems likely it also served another purpose. The preserved body made possible the return of the spirit during initiation rites.

Facing page: like the Egyptians, the Chinese filled their tombs with weapons, tools, and other articles. This 2100-year-old tomb, excavated in China, was filled with burial accessories.

Over left: a well-preserved mummy found by Egyptian archaeologists in a 2600-year-old tomb in Egypt is examined. Over right: carved in wood, is a statue that was found on top of the coffin in the burial chamber.

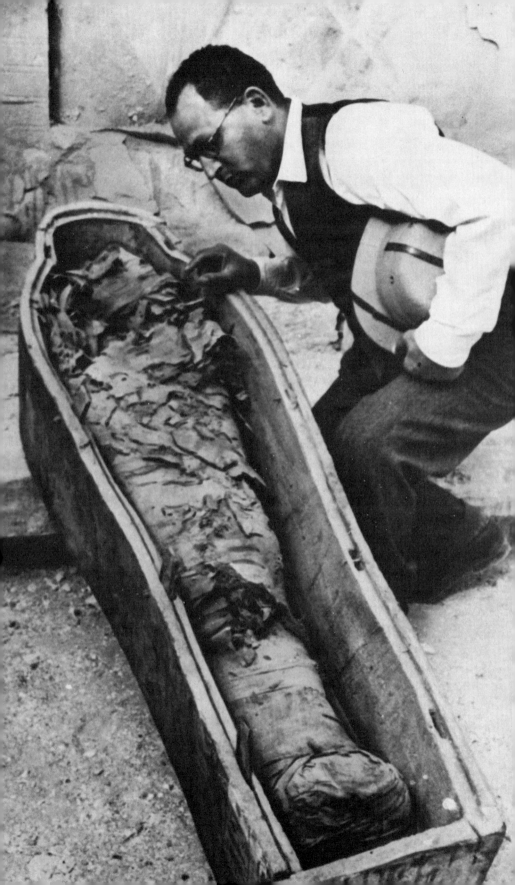

THE RITE OF INITIATION

There was a close connection between the Great Pyramid and the Egyptian mystery religions. Initiates were drawn from the spiritually adept who had shown a capacity to receive the secrets of life and death. As part of the newly imparted wisdom, the great laws of the cosmos and the principles of people's relation to it were conveyed to them with the strict understanding that they would not divulge these secrets. The highest degree of initiation was probably performed in the king's chamber where the body lay at rest.

Thus we see that the initiation rites enabled the pyramid to serve as *both* a tomb and a temple. While living, the adept were initiated into the life of the spirit. Upon death, the initiation was brought to its ultimate fulfillment.

According to a lifelong student of the subject, Manly P. Hall, the initiates "passed through the mystic passageways and chambers of the Great Pyramid, entering as mortals—albeit highly instructed mortals—to emerge as gods."

The 4,000-year-old tomb of King Tutankhamen is one of the greatest tourist attractions in the modern world. The mummy with its gem-studded gold mask and "pharaoh" headdress was found in this brown carved marble sarcophagus. The scene on the wall depicts the boy king (second figure from left) presenting his *Ka* (center) to Osiris, God of Death. The *Ka* carries the *ankh*, a looped cross symbol of life.

"The candidate," writes Hall, "was laid in the great stone coffer, which stood empty and uncovered as a symbol of resurrection, and for three days his spirit, freed from its mortal clay, wandered near the portals of immortality. His *ka,* or double, flew birdlike through the spiritual spheres of space, and he discovered that all the universe was a manifestation of life; all was progress; all was eternal growth and evolution. He realized that his body was a home which he could slip out of and return to without dying. Thus he achieved true immortality. At the end of three days he returned to himself again. Having personally experienced the great mystery, he was a true initiate—one who beheld and one to whom religion had fulfilled her duty by bringing him to the light of God."

One of the great mysteries of the thirty major pyramids is that no mummy has ever been found in one. This fact is usually attributed to the looting of thieves, although many of the pyramids showed no signs of having been opened until recent times. It is possible that the empty coffers in the Great Pyramid and others were a kind of baptismal font. The initiate may have been laid in them, to die symbolically and be born again, now to be revered as an adept or as a god.

According to Albert Champdor, a translator of *The Book of the Dead,* ". . . these massive examples of architecture were conceived to strike the populace with awe and to protect the small mortuary in which, before the mummified cadaver of the pharaoh, the profundities of an inviolable mystery, the rites of Osirisian resurrection, were performed."

A symbol of coming together of ascension to the heavens, and of the synthesis of all things, the pyramid is also the meeting place of two worlds—a magical world where funeral rites link mortal life to an after-life and allow human passage between the two, and a rational world comprised of geometry and architecture. With such a combination of mysticism and reason, the Great Pyramid offers a divine explanation of geometry and the justification of magic by mathematics.

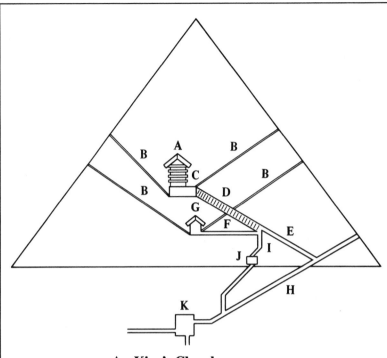

A. King's Chamber
B. Air Vents
C. Antechamber
D. Grand Gallery
E. Ascending Passage
F. Passage to Queen's Chamber
G. Queen's Chamber
H. Passage from Entrance
I. The Well
J. Small Room in Well
K. Underground Room

CROSS SECTION OF
THE GREAT PYRAMID

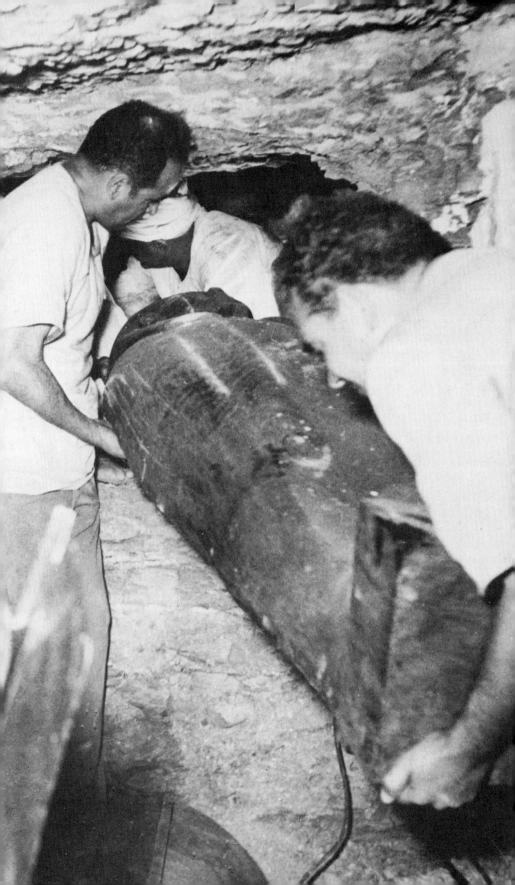

THE GEOMETRY OF
THE GREAT PYRAMID

The geometric proportions of the Great Pyramid provide many mysteries, including that of "squaring the circle." Imagine that we drop a plumb line from the top of the pyramid to its base. Having measured its height in this way, now imagine that its height is the radius of a circle, a circle which revolves around the top of the Great Pyramid like a wheel. We will find that the sum of the four base lines of the pyramid equals the circumference of our imaginary circle. Thus, the pyramid partakes also of the symbolic meaning of the circle, the wheel, and similar forms. The pyramidologists would see in this a solution to the problem of squaring the circle.

Actually, there is no geometrical way of squaring the circle because the value of *pi* (3.14159), which expresses the relationship between the diameter and the circumference, can never be exactly determined. However, squaring the circle is not a mathematical problem—it is an occult one. For thousands of years mathematicians have been trying unsuccessfully to solve it. They did not understand the symbolism of the problem. What then were the ancient Egyptians getting at?

The transforming of the square into a circle symbolizes the passage from earth to the heavens. The circle, according to the famous psychoanalyst Carl Jung, is an image of the total psyche, the symbol of being. The square is the symbol of earthly matter, of the body, and of reality. Thus, squaring

Near Cairo, this Egyptian sarcophagus was removed from the funeral chamber where it had rested undisturbed for twenty-five centuries.

the circle symbolizes the conflict between the spiritual transcendence, to which a person naturally aspires, and the earth where he or she is actually situated. The meaning of life lies in the passage from one state to the other.

But a further series of geometric relationships is also subject to interpretation. The four triangular faces of the pyramid correspond to the four elements which compose all living things: earth, air, fire, and water. The four elements ascend and are united at the summit. The summit symbolizes the fifth element, or spirit, symbolized by the circle. The dialectic of the square and the circle symbolizes the dialectic of earth and heaven, of the material and the spiritual.

J. E. Cirlot, in his *Dictionary of Symbols,* finds a contradiction between the pyramid as earth symbol and as fire symbol. "In the first place, in megalithic culture and in European folklores which have preserved its memory, the pyramid is symbolic of the earth in its maternal aspect. Pyramids with Christmas lights, moreover, express the twofold idea of death and immortality, both associated with the Great Mother. But this concerns the pyramid only insofar as it is a hollow mountain, the dwelling of ancestors and an earth-monument. The pyramid of stone, of regular geometrical shape, corresponds to fire, at any rate in the Far East." This contradiction, however, is more apparent than real.

This seeming contradiction disappears when the pyramid is seen as a synthesis of different forms, each with its own significance. The top of the pyramid is the Alpha and Omega, the beginning and the end of all things. The square base represents the earth, as we have seen. The triangular faces of the pyramid, joining the apex to the base, represent fire, divine revelation, and the threefold principle of creation. Consequently, the pyramid is not a simple but a complex form. It comprises two of the four basic forms (the triangle and the square) and is related to one other (the circle). Only a direct reference to the cross, the fourth basic form, is omitted.

Still further meaning may be found in contemplating the pyramid's complex symbolism. In the classic analysis of Manly P. Hall, "The square base of the pyramid is a constant reminder that the House of Wisdom is firmly founded upon Nature and her immutable laws." The Gnostics, a post-Christian philosophical and religious movement based in Egypt, claimed that their whole science rested on a square whose angles were silence, profundity, intelligence, and truth.

Manly P. Hall continues: "The sides of the Great Pyramid face the four cardinal angles, the latter signifying according to Eliphas Levi the extremities of light and darkness (east and west). The base of the pyramid further represents the four material elements or substances from the combinations of which the fourfold body of man is formed. From each side of the square there rises a triangle, typifying the threefold divine being enthroned within fourfold material nature. If each base line be considered a square from which ascends a threefold spiritual power, then the sum of the lines of the four faces (12) and the four hypothetical squares (16) constituting the base is 28, the sacred number of the lower world. If this be added to the three sevens composing the sun (21), it equals 49, the square of 7 and the number of the universe.

"The twelve signs of the zodiac, like the governors of the lower worlds, are symbolized by the twelve lines of the four triangles—the face of the pyramid. In the midst of each face is one of the beasts of Ezekiel, and the structure as a whole becomes the Cherubim. The three main chambers of the pyramid are related to the heart, the brain, and the generative system—the vital sources of energy and intelligence in the human constitution. The triangular form of the pyramid is also similar to the posture assumed by the body during the ancient meditative exercises. The Mysteries taught that the divine energies from the gods descended upon the top of the pyramid, which was likened to an inverted tree with its branches below and its roots at the apex. From this inverted tree the divine wisdom is disseminated by streaming down the diverging sides and radiating throughout the world." In other words, viewed as a temple, the pyramid is completed only by human participation. The initiate becomes the living apex through which divine power is focused into the diverging structure below.

If your mind is boggled at all by these symbols and the strangeness of occult thinking, you will soon become used to them. For the moment, just realize that the minds of our Egyptian ancestors were neither as simple nor as unsophisticated as many historians have supposed.

At this stage, we need to remember a few essential points. The complex symbolism of the pyramid arises from simple geometric proportions. After having studied these proportions, Matila Ghyka, in *Philosophy and Mysticism of Numbers,* concluded: "It is probable that the architect of the Great Pyramid was not conscious of all the geometric properties which we who have come later have discovered. Nevertheless, these properties are not accidental but flow almost organically from a conscious, governing idea expressed in the meridian triangle. The originality lies in the architect having captured a dynamic pulse in the abstract rigidity of the pyramid which could even be regarded as a mathematical symbol of organic life."

The phrase "organic life" well expresses the universal symbolism of the pyramid. The top of the pyramid symbolizes the Word, the first, engendering Power. Thus, at the summit of the ascending pyramid or spiritual ladder, the initiate attains union with the Word, just as the dead pharaoh in the hollow of the stone mountain was assimilated among the gods, the supreme and eternal end of all growing things.

THE HISTORY OF PYRAMIDOLOGY

The earliest European mention of the pyramids is probably the one found in the work of the Greek historian Herodotus (484–425 B.C.), "the father of history." When he visited Egypt, the four sides of the Great Pyramid were covered with polished casing stones which gleamed in the sunlight like mirrors. These stones were covered with inscriptions—all now lost to us. Herodotus was the first in a long line of wise men who, legend tells us, went to Egypt to study. Among others were Pythagoras, Plato, Archimedes, Aristotle, and Apollonius of Tyana. In ancient times, a person went to Egypt to acquire wisdom.

Despite this possible exchange with foreign scholars, Egyptian civilization failed to develop. With all their advances in civilization, it seems to have become almost a religious crime to change anything at all. After the Persian invasions, Egyptian culture began to fall apart. The long-kept secrets became more widely known. These secrets were scattered among different schools of thoughts. The Gnostics, the Jewish Kabbalists, and the Hermetic academies—all carried on parts of the occult tradition of Egypt.

Our knowledge of the occult wisdom embodied in the Great Pyramid is shrouded with lost secrets, contradictions, theories, and doubts. Many of our questions might be answered if we had the lost forty-seven volume *History* written by Strabo, a Pontine author and map-maker who lived in Egypt about 25 B.C. To make matters worse, the library at Alexandria, which contained so many of the now lost secrets, was burned twice.

Despite the efforts of early Christians to erase pagan beliefs, the Church itself became the storehouse of much of this forgotten lore. Much of the original wisdom had already seeped into Greek and Roman folklore. The Church, in its effort to convert the heathens, would adapt pagan myths to Christian purposes. In doing so, they unconsciously transferred much of the old occult knowledge into Europe. This knowledge went unnoticed by the faithful until the fall of Constantinople to the Turks in 1453, when the flight of Eastern scholars to Rome ushered in the Renaissance.

THE ARAB HISTORIANS

Our knowledge of the pyramids for almost a thousand years before the fall of Constantinople is dependent on Arab historians. In A.D. 640, the caliphs of Baghdad began stocking their libraries with manuscripts from all over the ancient world. Caliph Abdullah al Mamun, whose father Rashid inspired *Arabian Nights,* became pharaoh of Egypt in A.D. 813. He heard tales of the riches and the secrets of the universe stored in the Great Pyramid.

One tale in *Arabian Nights* tells of Al Mamun's quest and the fabulous treasure he found. Another story says that he found only enough treasure to pay a fair wage to his men. Still another story says that he found nothing at all and was forced to pay his men himself because he was afraid they would riot.

In the 1350s, descendants of Al Mamun decided to build a series of temples and mosques in Cairo. They stripped the polished casing stones from the Great Pyramid, removing 22 acres (8.9 hectares) of 100-inch (254-cm) slabs from the structure. The stones were dragged to Cairo to construct the mosque of Sultan Hassan.

Removing the casing stones exposed the granite blocks to sandstorms, rain, and wind. The elements began to destroy the Great Pyramid. Realizing this fact, the British astronomer and mathematician John Greaves set out in 1638 to measure the Great Pyramid before its proportions were lost. Greaves felt that the Great Pyramid might contain clues to the measurement of the earth. When he returned to England, his book *Pyramidographia* created a scientific sensation.

Sir Isaac Newton, the greatest of English physicists, studied Greaves' measurements. He decided that the pyramid had been built on a system of "sacred" and "profane" cubits. He determined that the sacred or Jewish cubit was between 24.80 and 25.02 inches (between 62.99 and 52.40 cm). He calculated the profane cubit was 20.63 inches (52.4 cm). Newton wrote a small book on the subject, *A dissertation upon the Sacred Cubit of the Jews and the Cubits of several Nations.*

Unfortunately, Greaves' measurements were incorrect. However, Newton went forward in his pursuit of a theory of gravitation. After a French astronomer obtained a precise figure for a degree of latitude, Newton reworked his findings and discovered his general theory of gravitation. Several ancient mathematicians had claimed that the measurements of the Great Pyramid were related to a geographical degree, and Newton agreed with them. From the precise siting of the Great Pyramid, it would seem the ancient builders did have knowledge of geographical degrees. Is it also possible that they understood gravitation?

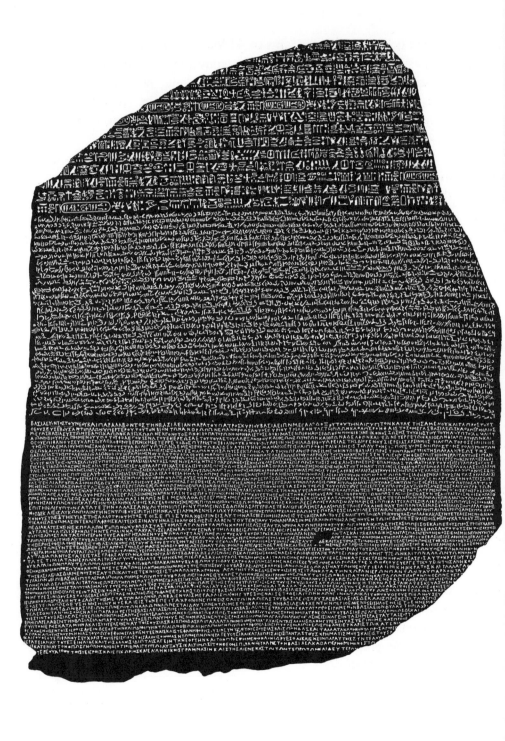

The next important investigation of the pyramids did not come from a scientist but from the great general, Napoleon Bonaparte. A captain in his Egyptian campaign discovered the famous Rosetta Stone on the Nile Delta. This yard-long (0.91 m) slab of stone was engraved with hieroglyphics and an ancient Egyptian language, neither of which could be deciphered—as well as one known language, Greek. The Stone was later captured by the British and placed in the Egyptian Department of the British Museum.

Except for a young French scholar, Jean-Francois Champollion, the hieroglyphics on the Stone baffled and then bored scientists. They could make nothing of it. After more than twenty years of study, Champollion succeeded in finding the answer to the secrets of Egyptian hieroglyphics. It was now possible to read and translate ancient Egyptian writings. The era of modern Egyptology had begun.

THE REDISCOVERY OF THE SECRETS OF THE GREAT PYRAMID

In 1765, Nathaniel Davison had discovered a hidden, 3-foot (.9-m) high room in the Great Pyramid. A few years after Champollion deciphered the Rosetta Stone, Captain G. B.

The discovery of the Rosetta Stone in Egypt in 1799 is considered to be one of the most important of all archaeological finds. The yard (.9 m) long slab of stone, cut in three languages—Greek, ancient Egyptian, and hieroglyphics, is now on display in the British Museum.

Caviglia, the master of a Maltese vessel, cleaned out the debris from Davison's chamber and set up housekeeping. Like so many others, he was convinced that a secret chamber existed in the pyramid. In 1836, Caviglia was joined by Colonel Howard Vyse, but the personalities of the two men clashed. After a tempestuous argument, Caviglia cleared his gear out and left the exploration to Vyse.

One of Vyse's contributions was the discovery of a chamber with five oblong royal inscriptions attributing the building of the Great Pyramid to Cheops. Vyse felt he had dated the construction period. He also established that the pyramid had originally been covered with casing stones. In 1840, Vyse returned home and wrote a book describing his explorations. The measurements taken by Vyse were the most precise until that date.

PYRAMIDOLOGY

At that time, England was being swept by the growing conflict between science and religion. John Taylor was among those who felt the conflict very deeply. He was the editor of *The Observer* in London, an astronomer, and an excellent mathematician. He never visited the Great Pyramid, but with the help of Vyse's assistants he built a scale model and studied its structure. Taylor recalled that Herodotus had written that the sides were scaled to equal the square of the pyramid's height. After much reasoning, Taylor divided the perimeter by twice the height of the pyramid and discovered that the Egyptians had been working with a value close to *pi*.

In addition, Taylor decided that Newton's sacred cubit was about 25 inches (63.5 cm) and based on the length of the earth's axis. He also found other curious units of measure in the pyramid. For example, he was struck by the figure 366, the number of days in the polar year. He also noted that the perimeter of the Great Pyramid measured very close to

36,600 British inches (92,964 cm). He also found that by dividing the base length by the sacred cubit he got a figure close to 366. How could the length of the earth's axis and other units of measure have been known to the ancient Egyptians?

It was inconceivable to Taylor that ancient knowledge was extensive enough to build the Great Pyramid. Divine intervention, he decided, provided the fantastic knowledge needed. The builders were members of a chosen race, who later founded the monotheism of Israel. Because the Egyptian unit of measure was so close to the inch used by the British, the people who settled the British Isles were related to the lost tribes of Israel. In 1864, Taylor published his findings in *The Great Pyramid: Why was it Built? And Who Built it?*

Impressed by Taylor's book, Charles Piazzi Smyth, Astronomer Royal for Scotland and a good mathematician, decided that he would go to Egypt and measure the Great Pyramid. Smyth solved one of Taylor's mathematical problems by inventing the "pyramid inch." Smyth based his inch on one part of a 25-inch (63.5-cm) casing stone. The results of his researches included the discovery that the base of the Great Pyramid divided by the width of a casing stone was exactly equal to 365—the number of days in the year. The pyramid inch, he found, was approximately one ten-millionth of the earth's polar axis. Smyth's 664-page work, *Our Inheritance in the Great Pyramid*, went through four editions (1864–1890). It was followed by two other works: the three-volume *Life and Work at the Great Pyramid* (1867) and *On the Antiquity of Intellectual Man* (1868).

With painstaking accuracy, Smyth applied the pyramid inch to every measurable portion of the pyramid. He wanted to see how many historical and scientific facts he could discover. For example, he found that if you multiply the height of the pyramid by ten to the ninth power, you obtain almost the distance of the sun from the earth. In the same manner, he discovered that the Great Pyramid encoded the earth's mean density, the mean temperature of the earth's surface, the period of the precession of its axis—all scientific facts only recently discovered. He then suggested a system of sacred measuring units which would replace the standard metric system. His "pyramid thermometer" used zero as the freezing point and a 50-degree mark based on the temperature of the king's chamber. The king's chamber is also on the fiftieth tier of the Great Pyramid.

Robert Menzies had advanced the theory that the Great Pyramid was a prophecy in stone. Humanity's history, he thought, is outlined symbolically in the passageways. Smyth extended this idea by inventing a chronological graph. Smyth felt that a year was equal to one pyramid inch and that the earth was created in 4004 B.C. The Great Flood, the Exodus were all coded into the pyramid's passageways. The beginning of the Grand Gallery marked Christ's birth.

One of Smyth's early followers, Joseph Seiss, was struck by the fact that the number five is the key number in the building of the Great Pyramid. It had five corners and five sides. The pyramid inch is one-fifth of one-fifth of a cubit. He also noted that we have five fingers and toes and five senses. There are five books of Moses and twice five precepts in the Decalogue. This intense fiveness in both nature and revelation, Seiss felt, could not have been accidental.

At this point, the reader who has seen an interpretation of symbols and the difficulties of occult reasoning in Chapter Two may be skeptical. Seiss is not really interpreting the number five as a symbol at all. He is merely applying it in ways that suit his convenience, in ways that prove what he wants it to prove.

If you and I were to set about measuring a complicated structure like the Great Pyramid, we would quickly have at our fingertips a mass of figures to deal with. If we were patient enough, we could eventually move them around so that we would find certain figures which matched up with important historical dates and scientific facts. Since we are bound by no rules except those we make up, is it surprising that our search for facts is successful?

But let us not become skeptical too soon. Certainly, any doubts you may have about pyramidology at this point are honest ones. Nevertheless, keep an open mind and put the facts to the test of your own experience.

We have seen that there are many remarkable and un-explained facts about the Great Pyramid. But does that mean that the whole of humanity's future has been coded in its mathematics? The mere design and building of the Great Pyramid is remarkable enough. Let us now glance briefly at the ways in which later pyramidologists have tried to explain the mystery of the Great Pyramid.

PYRAMID PROPHECY
AND THE ATLANTIANS

Since Charles Piazzi Smyth worked out the chronology of the Great Pyramid, it is not surprising that the first pyramid prophecies are found in his writing.

Taking the traditional thirty-three years of Christ's life, Smyth calculated the Lord's Atonement, his descent into Hell, and the final Resurrection. Continuing along the Grand Gallery, he discovered that the world was shortly to end. For Smyth, the twenty-nine year period between 1882 and 1911 was the Great Tribulation which was to precede the Second Coming of Christ. Clearly, this prophecy was not true. Perhaps Smyth had made some mistake in his reckonings?

His error was not immediately known to his contemporaries, though, and enthusiasm for pyramidology spread everywhere. In France, Abbé F. Moigno, Canon of St.-Denis, Paris, became a supporter, writing articles and spreading the word about pyramidology. In Britain, societies were formed by the dozens. They were going to try to change the British inch back into a unit based on the sacred Hebrew cubit. In Germany, a society of engineers met weekly to adapt Smyth's reckonings to current events.

It was in America, however, that the success of pyramidology reached its peak. In 1879 in Boston, citizens formed the International Institute for Preserving and Perfecting Weights and Measures. The reason for this society was to change the current measuring system to sacred pyramid cubits and to oppose the "atheistic" metric system used in France. President James Garfield was a strong member of the group, although he refused to serve on its board of directors.

Despite their confidence, the early pyramid prophets did not make many correct predictions. Today, it seems clear that if the Great Pyramid has any mysterious power, it is not the power of prophecy. But what about other powers—and how does the Great Pyramid come to possess them?

For early pyramidologists, the secrets of the pyramid could only be explained by divine intervention or by a mysterious people from outer space who landed on the lost continent of Atlantis.

Originally, the belief in Atlantis had only a vague connection with pyramidology. As the years passed, however, a lot of desperation was felt over the failure of the pyramid prophecies to come true. As a result, many people in the early part of this century began to seek other explanations for the mysteries of the Great Pyramid.

Many of these people found their answer in the belief that the Great Pyramid was built by Atlantians, not by Egyptians. They felt that the Great Pyramid represented the work of a civilization too advanced for any we know to have existed. They also noted that pyramids are to be found as far away from Egypt as South America, China, and even America.

The story of Atlantis begins with the Athenian philosopher Plato (427–347 B.C.). His book *Critias* contains our most complete record of Atlantis. According to this book, Atlantis was an island which stretched across the Atlantic from north Africa to the Caribbean. Atlantis was several days' sail from north Africa and was described as fertile, mountainous, with rolling plains watered by large rivers or canals. The people who lived there never had wars or other problems, and their civilization was far in advance of any other of that time—or perhaps even of our own time.

One source of Plato's knowledge of Atlantis was Solon, the wisest of the Seven Wise Men. He learned about Atlantis in Egypt. And as Plato repeatedly tells us, the memory of Atlantis disappeared among the Greeks because those who knew of it had died. Presumably, it was Critias the Younger who bequeathed the story of Atlantis to his nephew Plato.

According to the story handed down from Solon to Plato, Egyptian priests claimed that the Atlantian empire collapsed in a single day, in 9600 B.C., because of the arrogance and pride of its citizens. They were then engaged in attacking both Athens and Egypt. Their riches and the extension of their empire had led the Atlantians away from the true god and his laws. To punish them, he had caused an enormous volcanic eruption. Their continent split apart and sank beneath the waves of the Atlantic Ocean.

There are several flaws in this story. Athens did not exist in 9600 B.C. The writing and metal-working, which Plato said the Atlantians possessed, had not yet come into existence. Farming communities date from around 7000 B.C. Horses, which the people of Atlantis rode, were not known in Europe until the Bronze Age. Architecture of the kind Plato describes, including pyramids, did not exist before 4000 B.C.

The culture which Plato is describing is very like that of the High Bronze Age Civilizations of the Aegean and the Near East—such as the Minoan, the Mycenaean, the Hittite, the Babylonian, and the Egyptian. Was there something wrong with Plato's date? Had the Egyptian priests or Solon confused 900 with 9,000 years? If so, the date of the Atlantis disaster would be 1600 B.C. instead of 9600 B.C.

This notion makes the existence of Atlantis and its destruction much more believable. A volcanic explosion is known to have occurred during the Minoan empire in Crete in the sixteenth century B.C. The Minoan civilization fell because of a series of natural disasters, fires, floods, and earthquakes. Maybe a similar but more intense disaster occurred about the same time in the mid-Atlantic.

The godfather of modern Atlantian studies is Ignatius L. Donnelly, a Minnesota politician. His book *Atlantis: The Antedeluvian World* (1882) was the first book to bring together all the Atlantian evidence—including the central problem of the Great Pyramid. Donnelly cited numberless religious, mythological, folk, legendary, and scientific references to prove that Plato's lost continent was not a myth. It was a forgotten fact of world history.

Donnelly's basic ideas were simple. Atlantis was the true Garden of Eden, the source of all civilization. In a natural disaster, this island continent opposite the Strait of Gibralter sank beneath the ocean. Only a few of its inhabitants escaped by raft or boat. The tales of these survivors, Donnelly believed, came down to us in the form of flood legends. Such legends are common to almost all races and religions. As Atlantians scattered throughout the world, they brought their knowledge of advanced civilization with them.

The cross and the pyramid were objects of absorbing interest to Donnelly. The cross, he said, symbolizes the four rivers of the Garden of Eden and, thus, of Atlantis. He pointed to the worship of cross forms—even before Christianity. In a similar way, the pyramid symbolizes the mountain that stood in the midst of Eden—and in Atlantis. Donnelly pointed out the parallels among all pyramids, particularly between those in Egypt and Mexico.

A picturesque view of the Giza pyramids seen from the valley of the Nile.

Donnelly believed the pyramids of Mexico and Egypt were built for the same purpose. The orientation of the pyramid and the site chosen are always the same. In both Egypt and Mexico, the larger pyramids are dedicated to the sun, and the line through the middle is in the astronomical meridian. The Nile had a "valley of the dead," and in Teotihuacán (Mexico), there is a "street of the dead." In addition, the pyramids in both countries and throughout the world each have a small mound joined to one of their faces. Finally, the passageways inside are similar.

Who were these pyramid builders? The mystery is deepened by the presence of parallel structures around the world. Aerial photographs taken during World War II reveal a giant pyramid, encased in shimmering white stone and topped with a dazzling capstone in the Himalayas. Similar photographs were taken in 1947 of the mysterious Shensi pyramid in China. And then there are the massive earth pyramids in the United States, especially the Cahokia Mounds in Illinois. A similar structure, 170 feet (51.82 m) high and containing 1 million tons (900,000 metric tons) of earth, was built at Silbury Hill, England, over 4,000 years age.

There appears to be a world-wide system of pyramids. All around the world the characteristics of these pyramids are

In Mexico, the Great Pyramid of Chichén Itzá has characteristics similar to other pyramids around the world. This huge structure, once an important part of the vanished Mayan culture, is fifteen stories high, and resembles other pyramids in its architecture, masonry, and engineering.

similar. They are built on high places, and they parallel one another in their architecture, masonry, engineering, and astronomical orientation. Experts on Atlantis believe that at one time a people existed who had a technology so advanced that it is impossible for us to imagine it. For example, statues have been uncovered in South America depicting a variety of racial types. How could the natives of South America have known so many different types of people?

In addition, mummification and the other religious practices of all the pyramidal civilizations show a remarkable number of parallels. In fact, general cultural patterns of the pyramidal civilizations are similar. How could such a unification have come about?

Modern Atlantis theory has added to the early work of Donnelly, H.S. Bellamy, Egerton Sykes, Madame Blavatsky, and others. It is not concerned with proving the existence of Atlantis. These scholars consider that fact already established. They have tried to answer these questions. Who were the Atlantians? How could any civilization be so much more advanced than any others at that time? How could a unified, pyramidal culture come to exist throughout the world? Some believe it was because that culture did not develop from human culture at all. The people of Atlantis were extraterrestrial beings who brought their technology from outer space.

Among the numerous believers in this theory, the most recent and the most famous is Erich von Däniken. He has explored the Plain of Nazca in Peru, a country famous for its pyramids, and he has found a peculiar series of markings. According to von Däniken, in *Chariot of the Gods,* these markings parallel the aircraft parking areas in a modern airport. Other Atlantis experts point to the large number of drawings and sculptures which have been unearthed near the pyramids. They show people clothed and helmeted like modern fliers and astronauts.

Von Däniken's notion is that beings from another world introduced people to space travel during one of their ancient civilizations. As evidence, von Däniken points to a huge South American gate. On it are carvings which seem to relate to the orbit of Venus and to the Venusian calendar of 225 days. These stone carvings suggest to von Däniken that our ancestors may have come from Venus.

However, Venus makes only 6.48 orbits around the sun during a six day period. Thus, a Venusian would naturally describe the calendar as having six very long days. But to an earth person observing Venus, the time of the orbit would be 225 twenty-four-hour days. These carvings suggest that early people had knowledge of Venus' orbit but not its revolutions. Thus, the observer was almost certainly earth-bound.

Another notion is held by many Atlantis scholars. In their view, humanity could well have developed the technology for space travel and then lost it when civilization was destroyed by natural disasters. The survivors of these disasters slowly lost a clear memory of their past. What had once been known facts became distorted into legends. This view clearly holds on to more of the old Atlantis theories.

Which view, if either, do you like best? Either way, the evidence is very slight and we must rely on our intuition, or our hunches. Intuition is something we all have, and we all use it more often than we may be aware. My own intuition rejected the UFO theory, just as it rejected the standard textbook story of history. I simply feel that something is wrong with both of them. But we must each decide for ourselves what we feel about who built the pyramids and how and why.

Modern pyramidologists, however, are not very concerned with those questions. They are concerned with pyramid power, how it works, and how we can harness it to our benefit. We will begin learning about the secret power of the Great Pyramid in the next chapter.

PYRAMID POWER

Modern pyramidology began on the French Riviera in 1932. A twelve-year-old boy, Hubert Larcher, was walking through the streets of Nice. His eye was attracted to a strange display in a hardware store. It was a scale model of the Great Pyramid, under which was placed the dried-up remains of several small animals. The boy eventually grew up to become a famous parapsychologist and consulting physician to the French Ministry of Justice. Over the years, he continued to investigate the strange effects of pyramid power and to make others aware of them.

Antoine Bovis, the owner of the store, had become interested in mummification about 1920, when he visited the Great Pyramid. While walking around in the king's chamber, he found preserved bodies of bats, mice, cats, and other small animals that had wandered into the pyramid. Upon his return from Egypt, he constructed a scale model of the Great Pyramid and placed dead animals in it, about one-third of the way toward the apex from the base. This position was about that of the king's chamber. From this experiment, Bovis concluded that the shape of the pyramid prevented rapid decay and caused mummification.

Bovis believed that his experiments with the pyramid and other shapes had isolated mysterious and elusive powers. He called these powers radiethesia. He attributed different types of radiethesia to the sides of pyramids, squares, circles, funnels, and other forms. Apart from manufacturing his own patented pendulums, he gave talks and wrote about his ideas.

While still a young man, Hurbert Larcher wrote to the Czech engineer Karel Drbal (pronounced Dribble) and encouraged him to read the writings of Bovis. Drbal was skeptical, but he wrote to Bovis and later experimented with his own scale models. To his surprise, his experiments worked. He writes he was able to mummify "beef, calf, or lamb meat, eggs, flowers, and even dead reptiles such as frogs, snakes, lizards, etc."

Although the two men got along well, Drbal felt that Bovis was too magical for his standards. He claimed that Bovis was inclined to find radiations everywhere he used his pendulum. Eventually, the two men agreed to continue their experiments along separate paths.

Drbal had been a soldier in his youth. He recalled that, as a joke, soldiers would sometimes leave someone's razor in the moonlight. The moonlight would make the blade dull. Drbal expected the effect of pyramid power to be the same as the moonlight. However, dull blades were returned to their original sharpness. The average Gillette Blue Blade from which he once received five shaves now gave him fifty or more.

Drbal applied for a patent to manufacture his Cheops Pyramid Razor Blade Sharpener. He sold the American patent rights to Max Toth of New York. But after the publication of *Psychic Discoveries Behind the Iron Curtain,* by Sheila Ostrander and Lynn Schroeder, everyone began making pyramids.

Although Drbal might not have made much money from

his discovery, it created a sensation. Naturally, with more people thinking about pyramidology, more things began to happen. Old results were confirmed, and new effects of pyramid power were discovered. Max Toth and Greg Nielsen, in their book *Pyramid Power,* comment on several strange effects of pyramid power. Some people found that seeds placed inside a pyramid germinated more quickly and produced stronger, healthier plants in a shorter period of time than did untreated seeds.

Other people reported feeling better just by being near a model pyramid. Still other people reported that they placed a model pyramid near their beds. After several days or nights a specific pain or symptom disappeared or felt greatly better.

Another interesting observation was reported by many of the people who participated in these Toth experiments. When they raised their hands into the apex of the pyramid, they felt a prickling sensation, as if tiny needles were being stuck into them.

Just as Max Toth is the most important pyramidologist on the East Coast of the United States, G. Patrick Flanagan is the leading pyramidologist on the West Coast. A native of Glendale, California, Flanagan is a former boy prodigy in electronics. He holds more than two hundred patents on various inventions. He was cited with two full pages in *Life* magazine some years ago when they picked the one hundred most important young people in the country.

Flanagan is especially famous for developing an electronic device which enables deaf people to hear. This device changes sound into electrical impulses. These impulses are then sent directly to the brain which changes them back into sound. His Laser Stereo Conference System is a device which records voices exactly, regardless of how many people talk at once or how much noise there is around them. He is also interested in pyramids and the practical applications of pyramid energy. "It could provide the answer to the problem of hunger in the world," he explained. "We could store food substances such as grains indefinitely without fear of spoilage."

The author of several books, Flanagan is perhaps the most active and technically intelligent of the young people who are seeking practical ways of using pyramid power. He is already the inventor of several pyramidological devices, including the Pyramid Energy Generator. This device, he claims, will work anywhere and does not require a true alignment with the North Pole. It consists of fifteen 1-inch (2.54 cm.) pyramids with their own magnetic field built into the base.

WHAT IS "PYRAMID POWER?"

One of the main difficulties faced by Flanagan and others is the fact that we have only a vague idea of what pyramid power is or how it is generated. If we believe the evidence of pyramidologists, pyramid power works whether we understand it or not. Just as gravity worked before Newton brought us an understanding of it, so this force appears to work. Obviously, however, the practical applications of this force are limited by our lack of a theoretical understanding.

Karel Drbal has his own views on this problem. He compares the energy waves produced by the pyramid shape to the sound waves produced by the shape of a violin. Each violin produces its own particular tones, depending on its shape. "There's a relation," writes Drbal, "between the shape of the space inside the pyramid and the physical, chemical, and biological process going on inside that space." By using the right forms and shapes, Drbal believes we should be able to make processes occur faster or slower.

Pat Flanagan holds a similar view. He, too, feels that the pyramid acts as a sort of antenna, drawing various energies into itself. He feels that the Great Pyramid generates nanowave radiations by the simple fact that you have five corners. The radiation from the molecules and atoms of matter in the pyramid combine because of the angles of the corners. They form a beam of this radiation towards the middle of the pyramid.

Flanagan finds no conflict between pyramid power's life-giving force and its power to mummify. Death comes about because of decay. According to Flanagan, what could be more natural than a life-giving force resisting decay? "Biocosmic energy" is the term Flanagan coined for the apparent energy connected with the pyramid. The Russians call this energy "psychotronic" or "bioplasmic."

"This energy," writes Flanagan, "is the very essence of the life force itself. It has been known to exist, but until now no one has been able to isolate it." Before the scientific experiments of Flanagan and others, this force was called by many occult names—the Odic Force, Prana, Mana, Etheric Force, Kundalini, Animal Magnetism, Ki, or Chi, depending on the time and place of the culture which gave it birth.

If we were to search through the thousands of books on the subject, we could find certain characteristics of this force which remain the same in all times and places. Apparently these energies are all one and the same. Today, we call it pyramid power. Even our English word "pyramid" comes from the Greek word *pyro,* which means fire or heat. The Greek word *mesos* means at or near the middle. *Pyramid means fire in the middle.* The very form of the pyramid is an expression of the life-giving force.

We are not certain of the differences between pyramid force and other known forms of energy, such as electromagnetic and atomic. Scientists are aware that there are many more forms of energy in the universe than the few we now know about. Every hundred years or so, we discover a new source of energy. Each discovery brings us closer to that basic energy from which all others derive.

What appears to be the major difference between pyramid power and known forms of energy has been well expressed by Dr. Elmer Green, director of the Psychophysiological Laboratory at the Menninger Foundation. He writes that in occult physics there is a notion of energy remarkably similar to that of modern physics. In both subjects, there is one primary form of energy from which everything else is constructed. In occult physics, however, it is believed that the one basic energy includes more than just physical substance. It also includes emotional and mental substance. In the human being all these substances are brought together.

PYRAMID POWER IN PRACTICE

Research in pyramidology is being carried on all over the world, from Moscow to Los Angeles, from Toronto to Johannesburg. The experimenters are as varied as can be imagined. They include full-time scientists and outright rascals, professional psychics and curious amateurs. Current research is so varied that we will consider only a few of the more evidential experiments and the more respected research establishments.

LIQUIDS

Some of the earliest and most important experiments with pyramid power were performed with liquids. Bill Schul and Ed Pettit filled and covered two identical containers with freshly homogenized milk. They placed one inside a pyramid and the other just outside it. The one outside the pyramid is known as the control subject because it is not exposed to any special influences.

Six days later the milk in the pyramid had turned into layers of curds, so did the milk on the outside, but not as much, and mold had begun to form. A few days later the mold had grown so thick on the milk that it was thrown away. Six weeks later, the milk in the pyramid had developed no apparent mold. It had settled into a solid, creamy, smooth substance which tasted like yogurt.

Repeated tests were made, but the results varied. At times, the pyramid milk did not turn to yogurt but simply separated into layers. They were not able to determine what caused the different results. The difference may have been due to variations in temperature and humidity, although they tried to keep these the same. Also, they suspect that the seasons, changes in the moon, varying cosmic radiation, and so on could have affected the experiments. Judging from Dr. Alvarez's experiences in measuring cosmic radiation, the energy fields within the pyramid change from time to time for unknown reasons.

When you begin your own experiments, you might want to duplicate this one by Schul and Pettit. If you do, study this experiment carefully. Notice how they tried to *keep conditions exactly the same for both the milk container in the pyramid and the control container outside it.* Try to design your experiment so that the pyramid is the only variation. With every element the same for both containers, you should get identical results. With the pyramid as the only difference, any difference in your results may be attributed to pyramid power.

In another experiment, James Raymond Wolfe "charged" I pint (.48 l) of water by leaving it within a pyramid for three weeks. A control pint was left outside for the same period of time. Wolfe took elaborate precautions against error and any unconscious bias on his part. To begin with, both containers were covered in exactly the same way. Sixteen 2-ounce (56.7 gram) plastic vials were obtained from a pharmacy. The same number of well-used ($1) bills were obtained from a bank. The last three serial numbers on each were copied on each of the vial caps.

In Wolfe's absence, an assistant filled eight of the vials from the pyramid water and eight from the control water. Picking caps at random from within a paper bag, she sealed all of the vials. Then she recorded the numbers of those containing the pyramid water. This provided Wolfe with a coded system in which no set of numbers could be connected with any other.

This procedure is known as "randomizing" your experiment. It prevents any unconscious "fudging" with the results.

To complete his experiment, Wolfe began to water sixteen groups of sunflower seeds. Each group was numbered and always watered from the same vial. Soon, eight of the seed packet groups were growing more quickly than the others. The results? "In every case," says Wolfe, "of early growth, the seed was identified as having been watered from the pyramid-charged supply."

Of course, some seed packets contain healthier seeds than others. These would naturally grow faster. However, the experimenter has no way of knowing which packet contains the healthiest seeds. It is also possible that the eight healthier seed packets found their way into the pyramid group by accident. However, the odds against such an accident are astronomical.

To confirm the results of Wolfe's experiment, you would need to repeat it several times. His experiment has not been followed up as it should have been. For this reason, you might find it especially attractive to try to duplicate his results. It is one of the most remarkable and convincing experiments in pyramid power.

PLANTS

One of the most frequently used subjects for the testing of pyramid power is plant life. However, because of the Loehr and Backster experiments, it is very difficult to conduct a test with flowers. Franklin Loehr is credited with having discovered the "power-of-prayer-on-plants." In fact, he merely established in the public mind what had been known for centuries. During my years at the Parapsychology Foundation, we experimented with a Hungarian psychic, Estebany. He could make a particular plant grow faster, more healthy, and live longer than another. Experiments with other psychics tended to produce the same results either through prayer, meditation, or simply touching the plant over a period of time.

I first heard Cleve Backster speak in Chicago at a meeting of the Spiritual Frontiers Fellowship. I was frankly skeptical. It was not his results I was skeptical about but his methods. I did not believe that you could measure the response of plants to human feelings by electronic instruments. However, his results have now been duplicated by so many people using similar methods, it is difficult not to accept his experiments.

Anyone who loves flowers will tell you that they are living beings and sense and respond to a person's mood just as a dog or cat will. For the scientific community, however, the Loehr and Backster discovery came as a breakthrough. For pyramidology, it is just another problem. How do you invent a control that will rule out the "Loehr–Backster effect?" In other words, how do you know when the effects on the plants are the results of your feelings and when they are the result of a force created by the pyramid? To date, no totally successful experiment has been devised. If you decide you want to test pyramid power on your plant, you might try wrestling with the problem yourself.

One interesting experiment was performed by Jules Green of the Psychical Research Society, Philadelphia. You might want to try to duplicate his experiment. To begin, buy four fresh flowers. They can be any flowers, but let us suppose that they are roses. Cut their stems to make them as nearly as possible the same length. Weigh them.

Place the roses in four different places. One should be in

the open air. If possible, one should be in a commercially made pyramid and another in one you made yourself. One should be placed in a cube which you have made with a volume equal to that of the two pyramids.

Each rose should be placed under the geometric center of its container, and the flower should be pointed toward the magnetic north. The flower that is left in the open should also be placed so that the petals face north. Four other flowers should be placed in the same way. Let us suppose that they are tulips. The experiments should now be put away on a pantry shelf. There they will be protected from temperature changes and other variables. Do not look at them or open the pantry door for a week.

At the end of that time, Jules Green found the flowers in the cube and the pyramids were still fresh. The ones which had been left in the open had withered. He found the same results for the tulips. At first, Green could not understand why the flowers in the cubes should be as fresh as those in the pyramids. It was only after he inspected them more carefully that he realized the roses and the tulips in the pyramids *had grown*. Otherwise, they were the same as the flowers in the cubes.

Bovis had experimented not only with pyramids, but with cubes, cones, and other shapes. The results of these different experiments would be interesting, but unfortunately Bovis' papers and notes have long since disappeared. As a result, a great deal of his experimentation needs to be repeated. Before that can be done, however, more people will have to test pyramid power with carefully designed experiments.

Designing an experiment is not as simple a matter as it may seem. You don't throw a piece of raw meat in a pyramid and wait to see what happens. In a later chapter, we will take a look at the important do's and don'ts that must be followed if an experiment is to be a success.

SOLIDS

Certain metals, such as gold and silver, are extremely receptive to pyramidal influence. For example, tarnish is much more quickly removed from jewelry and old coins in pyramid-treated water than in untreated water. Aluminum, on the other hand, seems at first unaffected by pyramid power. Plants surrounded by an aluminum shield fail to react when placed in a pyramid. Seeds placed on aluminum begin to grow less quickly than those treated with plain water but placed on another seed bed.

Aluminum is an element extracted from a mineral made by an electrical process. Magnets have similar negative effects on pyramid power. But that is because they create an overdose of pyramidal force. One of two things may be happening: (1) the aluminum resists pyramid power; (2) it joins with electromagnetic forces to produce an additional charge.

Various experimenters found that the blocking action of aluminum was overcome when the metal was left inside a pyramid for two weeks or longer. The growth and movement of plants was no longer blocked by the aluminum. But what was more astonishing in these experiments was that the foil itself seemed to act as a kind of pyramid.

Seeds placed on the aluminum which had been exposed inside a pyramid began to grow as quickly as those within the pyramid. Plants exhibited the same results. Beef wrapped in treated aluminum and cooked under identical conditions, cooked in one-third the time of beef wrapped in regular foil.

The answer to this phenomena is not entirely clear. One notion is that the electrical qualities in the atoms of the aluminum absorb the pyramidal energy very slowly. Thus they release it very slowly. That is to say, when the foil is removed from the pyramid, the atoms no longer have an outside energy source. The electron's orbit begins a process of slow decay. As a result, the foil releases energy and can be used as a substitute pyramid. However, this is only one notion and much more experimentation needs to be done with aluminum.

Karel Drbal's experiment with razor blades has been duplicated by thousands of people, myself included. It is perhaps the most famous of all the experiments with pyramid power and the one which made pyramidology so popular.

To carry out this series of experiments, you must build cardboard pyramids which reproduce the proportions of the Great Pyramid. Follow the instructions which will be given to you in the last chapter of this book. If you can find them, use the single-edged Gem brand of blades. They do not have any edge coating such as platinum or stainless steel which might interfere with your experiment. If you cannot find Gem blades, then any of the standard double-edged blades will do. You will need two blades. Place blade A on the platform inside the pyramid and blade B in the open air as a control.

Just before the experiment, take both blades and dull them by stroking each ten times through the bristles of a toothbrush. Use the same pressure on each stroke. Then place the blades on a shelf and leave them undisturbed for seven days. Place both blades pointing toward the magnetic north.

After seven days, remove the blades and mark one of them so that you will be able to tell them apart. If you don't shave, ask your father or older brother to help you with the experiment. He should shave one side of his face with one blade and one side with the other. Don't tell him which blade is the one which has been exposed to pyramid power.

Whether your first experiment is a success or not, you will need to repeat the experiment about ten times before you can arrive at any results. In the first place, even though both blades come from the same package, one may be duller than another. There is no way you can control this—so repeat your experiment and note the results.

There is also a psychological problem. How dull is dull when a person considers a blade too dull to shave with? Every person's judgment will be different. This is another reason why you must run a number of experiments.

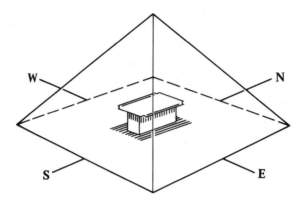

W N

S E

**Razor blade in pyramid, showing
also the position of the platform
in the center of the pyramid
so that the top of the platform is
one-third of the distance
from the base to the apex.**

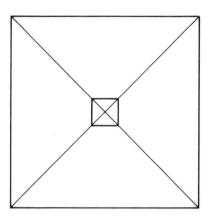

**Platform seen from above,
showing its position directly under
the apex of the pyramid**

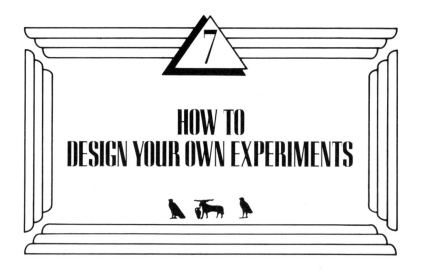

HOW TO
DESIGN YOUR OWN EXPERIMENTS

Patience is the first requirement for any type of experimentation. It is doubly important in a new subject like pyramidology. Impatience and the expectation of quick results will lead to discouragement.

Be critical—both of your results and of yourself. Ask yourself at all times whether you are remaining objective about what you are doing. This objectivity is especially necessary when you are evaluating your results. Don't be carried away. A successful experiment requires more than carrying out rules and procedures. It requires that you be patient and honest with yourself.

Be precise. Even the best thought out experiment can be ruined if it is done hastily or carelessly. If your early experiments are unsuccessful, analyze what you have done. Check to make sure that the measurements of your pyramid are correct, that you have properly lined up both your pyramid and your specimen. Ask yourself if you have kept your specimen long enough and have observed the proper controls.

Even when you feel that you have done everything possible in an unsuccessful experiment, do not give up. Do exactly what you must do if the experiment had proved to be a success. Repeat it!

One or two experiments prove nothing either way. And remember that even when an experiment fails, it may prove to be a success. The failure may be due to something which you had not considered before and which you can correct. In that case you will learn something. The failure may be due to something no previous experimenter has noticed. In that case, you will have made a valuable contribution to pyramidology.

So far we have only mentioned the basic emotional elements in experimentation. They are no less important than the objective procedures which will follow. A good example is the man who was asked to explain his results. He replied, "Well, I set a row of seeds. Then as the first ones come up, I pop a pyramid over them." Since the healthiest and strongest plants will naturally come up first, he is determining the results of his experiment from the beginning!

Emotional elements such as these will ruin even the best experiment. Nevertheless, there are certain controls which will help to get rid of self-deception. Among the basic controls are these:

1. Your specimen and your control specimen must be as nearly identical as you can make them.

2. Your specimen and your control specimen must be kept under the same circumstances. The only element in the experiment which should make any difference in the results must be the pyramid itself.

3. The experiment must be repeatable. A good idea is to decide on a series of ten run-throughs. Repeat your experiment ten times and keep a careful record of the results. Repeat this procedure for another run of ten. Then evaluate your results—judge your successes against your failures. If you have kept the conditions the same for both runs, you should achieve about the same results in both runs. Let us say, seven successes against three failures on the first run; six successes against

four failures on the second run. If there is any wider variance, you know something is wrong.

4. The experiment must be verifiable by someone else. If you are the only person who can perform the experiment, then you know that something is very definitely wrong. Have a friend perform the experiment at the same time. See if he or she can repeat your experiment independently. In either event, do not discuss your experiments with each other while they are in progress. Do not try to influence one another.

When you follow these guidelines, you will be using the basic principles of the scientific method. In duplicating the experiments described in this book, you will be learning to master methods that are used in all the sciences. After you have achieved some results on your own, you might even want to ask your science teacher if you can repeat your experiment at school.

If you are not successful, you may want to take your experiment to your science teacher and ask what you are doing wrong. And most important, when you have duplicated the experiments described in this book, you will want to begin to make up your own experiments. Your science teacher can be a great help. Following the methods you have learned in this book, design your own experiment at home and then bring it to school for suggestions.

My own first experiments were done with razor blades, and I had to perform them on my own. No one would take me seriously. The experiments were highly successful. Finally, the friend who had made the most fun of my experiments decided he was going to check me out. He did. And he got the same results!

Although he was still unconvinced, we decided to try more complex specimens than razor blades. We decided we would experiment with fresh hamburger meat (which can be a little costly) and that we would both follow the procedures outlined on the following page:

1. We weighed our specimens before placing them in separate pyramids. To determine the dehydration rate for each specimen, we would reweigh it each day until it had totally dehydrated.

2. We each set up two other containers—a clean tin can and a small cardboard box (rectangular). Both were identical. Each had a volume equal to that of the pyramid. The boxes had covers; the tin cans did not. In each control container we put a specimen of hamburger nearly identical to that in the pyramid. (The hamburger had all been purchased at the same time from the same butcher.) These specimens were also weighed each day and at the same time. After each weighing, the specimens were restored to exactly the same position in their containers.

3. Then we each placed an identical specimen in the open air on flat pieces of wax paper. These, too, were weighed each day.

4. We each started a daily record of our progress. In this record we noted the following facts regarding the meat: composition, dimensions of each specimen, the shape and volume of each container, the date and hour when the meat was purchased. Each day we recorded the weight of each specimen. We recorded any visible changes in firmness, texture, discoloration, lack of moisture, and decay. We entered our records at the same time each day and dated the entries.

At first everything went well. The pyramid-treated meat achieved dehydration sooner in both of our experiments. After the first test, the results began to vary wildly. There was no consistency in the results I was getting. There was none in the results my friend was getting. What is more, there was no consistency between our results. In one test, his pyramid-treated meat would dehydrate, while mine would rot. In the next test the results would be reversed. And yet we were using exactly the same meat.

We each performed 10 tests, 20 separate tests in all. And try as we would, going over our log books, no consistency, no pattern emerged in our results. Then we realized our mistake. We had thought of using hamburger because it was cheap and because we could mold the specimens so that they would be identical. But, of course, the strands of hamburger do not necessarily come from the same slab of meat or even from the same animal.

What we had not considered was that most commercial food, even so-called fresh meat, has been processed and that chemical preservatives have been added. Obviously, these chemicals will affect the dehydration rate and invalidate the experiment. Hamburger was probably the worst meat we could have chosen. We were both disappointed at the enormous waste of time and effort, but we had learned something.

When experimenting with any form of food, you may follow our general procedures, but use only those foods which are free of preservatives. Make sure fruit or vegetables are organically grown. We experimented later with organically grown tomatoes, and the results were favorable.

Even when all precautions have been taken, do not expect uniform results. The dehydration process itself allows for variables. The shrinking or shriveling of a specimen depends on the ratio of water to fiber content. The higher the ratio of moisture to fiber the more misshapen the specimen will become. Among flowers, roses make good specimens. They have a low moisture-high fiber ratio and will dehydrate almost perfectly. However, no two roses are the same. Repeat the experiment a number of times.

If you are performing your first experiments with pyramid power, I would suggest staying away from biological specimens. Experiments of this kind are very hard to control and evaluate. There are so many variables in biological tests— moisture, sunlight, air, identical growing conditions, as well as the problem of finding identical specimens—all these factors have to be overcome if the experiment is to be wholly successful. Even two peas in a pod will produce pea pods whose size varies.

It is probably best to begin with something inorganic and simple—like a razor blade. If the results encourage you, move on to more complex specimens. But always remember to check your controls—and use your imagination. We have left this vital element for the last. Imagination—no experiment is of high value without it. In the beginning, duplicate the experiments of others, partly to convince yourself that pyramid power works and partly to gain experience. But as you progress in the subject, you will naturally want to use your imagination and do things no experimenter has done before.

But how does one begin without a pyramid? Actually, it is very easy to make your own pyramid, and the various methods of doing so can be described very briefly.

HOW TO
BUILD YOUR OWN PYRAMID

Of course, you can buy a commercially made pyramid, but that is not advisable. In the first place, it costs a great deal more than to make one of your own. And in the second place, if you send away for a pyramid, you may not get what you ordered or exactly what was advertised.

Pyramid models vary in style, size, and materials. They may vary from a few inches to several feet, depending on the size of your specimen—including you, should you care to use it for meditation. Excluding all metals, especially aluminum, current research indicates that the material used in building the pyramid does not greatly affect the results. The smaller pyramids are usually made from cardboard or wood. The larger ones are usually made from wood, fiberglass, or plastic sheeting. The important point is to avoid using metal as much as you can. Metal seems to inhibit and enhance the electromagnetic properties in the pyramid force. Use wooden dowels and glue instead of nails.

The size, as we have said, is determined by the specimen. For razor blades, the pyramid need be no more than 4 inches

(10.16 cm) from the apex to the base. For plant seedlings, about 18 inches (45.72 cm) is sufficient. (Give them room to grow!) To accommodate 1 gallon (3.79 l) of water, the pyramid should be about 3 to 4 feet (.914–1.219 m) tall. For a meditating person, either sitting or lying down, it should be about 6 feet (4.876 m) high.

A floor base is not required. However, a base does add to the stability and to the accuracy of alignment. If the pyramid is made of firm materials, it will be simplest to cut a door in one side and hinge it. If made of flimsy material, simply make a flap which you can pull closed and fasten.

If you want to be a purist, use compressed cardboard instead of corrugated cardboard. Avoid plywood and use solid woods instead. If you want to use plastic, make sure it is a styrene plastic, not styrofoam.

THE DIMENSIONS

If your mathematical or mechanical ability is somewhat limited, or if you lack certain tools or materials—don't worry. Your limitations are no greater than mine, and I have made several successful pyramids. Simply follow the instructions given in the diagrams on pages 75 and 76.

Once you have decided on the height and material, consult the chart on the opposite page.

If you want to begin measuring in feet, the proportions are now very simple.

HEIGHT

1 foot (.3048 m)

BASE

1.5708 feet (.4788 m)

SIDE

1.495 feet (.4557 m)

HEIGHT	BASE	SIDE
1 inch (2.54 cm)	1.57 inches (3.99 cm)	1.495 inches (3.78 cm)
2 inches (5.08 ″)	3.14 ″ (5.44 ″)	2.99 ″ (7.59 ″)
3 ″ (7.62 ″)	4.71 ″ (11.96 ″)	4.485 ″ (11.39 ″)
4 ″ (10.16 ″)	6.28 ″ (15.95 ″)	5.98 ″ (14.43 ″)
5 ″ (12.70 ″)	7.85 ″ (19.94 ″)	7.475 ″ (18.97 ″)
6 ″ (15.24 ″)	9.42 ″ (23.93 ″)	8.97 ″ (22.81 ″)
7 ″ (17.78 ″)	10.99 ″ (27.91 ″)	10.465 ″ (26.58 ″)
8 ″ (20.32 ″)	12.56 ″ (31.93 ″)	11.96 ″ (30.38 ″)
9 ″ (22.86 ″)	14.13 ″ (35.92 ″)	13.455 ″ (34.18 ″)
10 ″ (25.40 ″)	15.70 ″ (39.88 ″)	14.95 ″ (37.97 ″)
11 ″ (27.94 ″)	17.27 ″ (43.87 ″)	16.445 ″ (41.77 ″)
12 ″ (30.48 ″)	18.84 ″ (47.88 ″)	17.94 ″ (45.57 ″)

If you want, let us say, a 3-foot, 3-inch (.9906 m) height to your pyramid, multiply the above base and side by three. That will give you your measurement in terms of feet. Mark that length off. Then consult your table for inch proportions. You will find that you must add 4.71 inches (11.96 cm) to the base and 4.485 inches (11.39 cm) to the sides of the footage you have already marked off.

It is very important that the sides form an angle to the base of 51 degrees, 52 minutes, and 10 seconds. If you follow the above proportions you will have an exact replica of the Great Pyramid.

To align your pyramid properly, use a compass to determine the magnetic north. Draw a straight line through the middle of your pyramid and place it so that the line is facing in the same direction as your compass needle.

Make sure that the pyramid is placed away from all electrical equipment such as radios, televisions, light sockets, and so forth. Keep the pyramid as far away from any metal objects as possible. In winter this may prove difficult to do.

When constructing the platform for your specimens, make sure that it is one-third the height of the pyramid from the base. You can construct the platform from any material you prefer except metal. It should be removable so that it may be cleaned after each experiment.

When placing the specimen on the platform, be sure that the longest portion of it is on a north-south axis. The control specimen should, of course, be placed in a similar manner. If the specimen is circular, place it directly under the apex.

The atmosphere surrounding the pyramid should be relatively constant with regard to humidity and temperature.

Test your pyramid from time to time for the amount of energy rising from the apex. To do so, you may use either a pendulum or a dowsing rod.

A pendulum may be made from any small but heavy object. A ring or metal nut attached to a string will do. While

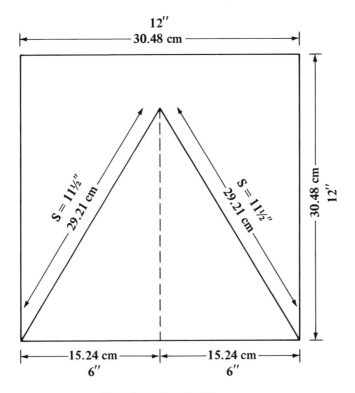

FIRST METHOD

You can make a pyramid by using four sheets of cardboard. Take a ruler and pencil and draw an equal-sided triangle on the cardboard. For example, if you want a pyramid approximately 8 inches (20.32 cm) high, you would need four pieces of cardboard 12 inches (30.48 cm) square.

Use a compass that has an opening of at least 12 inches (30.48 cm). Set the compass at 11 1/2 inches (29.21 cm) and place the point at the lower left-hand corner and draw an arc. Then with the point of the compass set at the lower right-hand corner draw another arc. Where the arcs intersect is the apex of the triangle. Repeat this process on each of the four sheets of cardboard. Draw the sides from the intersection to the bottom corners of your triangles. Cut the triangles from your cardboard and tape them together.

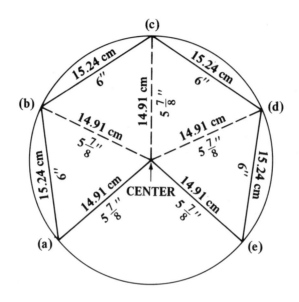

SECOND METHOD

To construct a pyramid in one piece, study the above diagram, then take your compass and draw a circle 5 7/8 inches (14.91 cm) in radius. Then draw a line from the center (where you placed the point of your compass) to point (a) on the circle. Use your ruler and draw a line from the center to point (a). Placing the point of your compass at (a), set it for 6 inches (15.24 cm) and mark off a 6-inch (15.24-cm) length on the rim of the circle, point (b). Place the point of the compass at point (b) and proceed in a similar manner and mark off point (c). Continue in the same way and mark off points (d) and (e).

With your ruler, connect each of the five points with one another and with the center. Using a dull knife, score along the dotted lines from the center to points (b), (c), and (d). Now cut the two remaining lines (a and e) and fold along the scored or dotted lines. Tape the edges together. You now have a pyramid approximately 4 inches (10.6 cm) high.

For pyramids of other sizes, see chart on page 73.

holding the string, move slowly toward the pyramid and suspend it over the apex. Hold it there until it ceases to move. Then try to keep it motionless. If the pyramid is emitting energy, the pendulum will swing in one direction or the other or will begin to make slow circles around the apex.

To determine the strength of the pyramidal energy being emitted, raise the pendulum successively higher. Pyramid power is believed to rise in a spiral from the apex, widening and dispersing itself as it rises. The pendulum should react less the farther away from the apex it is.

The best dowsing rod is a forked hazel stick, if you can find one. Grip each fork lightly in your hand. As you approach the apex of the pyramid, you will feel the stem tug downward, perhaps even begin to bend downward in your hands.

Since most people do not live near a hazel tree, it will probably prove simpler and easier to straighten out two coat hangers. Bend them so that about 7 inches (17.78 cm) of each is at a 90-degree angle from the handles. As with the pendulum, move slowly toward the pyramid's apex. The 7-inch handles should be held parallel to each other. The 30-inch (76.20 cm) prongs should be held parallel to each other and away from you. Grasp them gently so that they will be able to respond to the energy being emitted from the apex of the pyramid.

Hold the rods so that they bracket the pyramid *above* the apex. If energy is being emitted in sufficient force, the rods will either cross over one another, forming an X, or they will begin pointing away from each other.

In conclusion, we might reconsider some of the speculations which the Great Pyramid at Giza has raised.

It is a clue to a new form of energy.

It is our link to the stars.

Like the Akashic Record of the Hindus, the Great Pyramid is the history of all that humanity has ever done, a library of forgotten lore.

The Great Pyramid is a model of the universe.

The Great Pyramid is our key to finding the lost continent of Atlantis.

The Great Pyramid was created by extraterrestrial beings monitoring the earth.

The Great Pyramid was built by the ancient Egyptians.

The Great Pyramid is the history of our future.

The Great Pyramid is an occult rendering in stone of humanity's spiritual journey through life.

These are but a few of the speculations, expressed and unexpressed, which we have touched upon in this book. They are some of the speculations which the Great Pyramid continues to evoke. Are any of them true? Are all of them true to some extent? We must make up our own minds. What remains true is that the Great Pyramid continues to mystify the minds and excite the imaginations of people everywhere.

BIBLIOGRAPHY

Here are some books for further reading. They all contain more information about the pyramids and pyramidology. Those marked with an * are available in paperback editions. The others you will be able to find in most libraries.

Brunton, Paul. *A Search in Secret Egypt*. London: Rider, 1936.

* Charroux, Robert. *One Hundred Thousand Years of Man's Unknown History*. New York: Berkley Books, 1970.

Davidson, David. *The Great Pyramid: Its Divine Message*. London: William & Norgate, 1924.

* Ebon, Martin, Ed. *Mysterious Pyramid Power*. New York: New American Library, 1976.

Gardner, Martin. *The Incredible Dr. Matrix*. New York: Charles Scribner's, 1976.

Hall, Manly, P. *The Secret Teachings of All Ages*. Los Angeles: Philosophical Research Society, 1969.

* Loehr, F. *The Power of Prayer on Plants*. New York: New American Library, 1969.

* Michell, J. *The View Over Atlantis*. New York: Ballantine Books, 1969.
* Ostrander, S. and Schroder, L. *Psychic Discoveries Behind the Iron Curtain*. Englewood Cliffs, N.J.: Prentice-Hall, 1970.
  Proctor, R. H. *The Great Pyramid: Observatory, Tomb, and Temple*. London: Chatto & Windus, 1883.
* Seiss, J. A. *The Great Pyramid: A Miracle in Stone*. New York: Rudolf Steiner Publications, 1973.
* Schul, Bill and Pettit, Ed. *The Secret Power of the Pyramids*. New York: Fawcett, 1975.
* Smith, Warren. *The Secret Forces of the Pyramids*. New York: Zebra Books, 1975.
  Smyth, Charles Piazzi. *New Measures of the Great Pyramid*. London: R. Banks, 1884.
  Taylor, John. *The Great Pyramid: Why Was It Built? and Who Built It?* London: Longmans Green, 1863.
* Tompkins, Peter. *Secrets of the Great Pyramid*. New York: Harper and Row, 1971.
* Toth, Max and Nielsen, Greg. *Pyramid Power*. New York: Freeway Press, 1974.
* Valentine, Tom. *The Great Pyramid*. New York: Pinnacle Books, 1975.
* Von Däniken, E. *Chariots of the Gods*. London: Souvenir Books, 1969.
  Watson, L. *Super Nature*. New York: Doubleday, 1973.

INDEX

Drbal, Karel, 50–51, 52, 61

Earth data, relationship to pyramid measurements, 34, 35–36
Egyptian Book of the Dead, 15, 22
Egypt: pyramids, 11–12, 21–22, 40, 42, 45; religion, 11–12, 15–16, 21–22, 29
Energy, forms of, 52–54, 77
Etheric Force, 53
European Occult Research Society, 2
Extraterrestrial visitors, as pyramid builders, 46–47, 78

Flanagan, G. Patrick, 51–53
Flood legends, 36, 42
"Four Elements," 26, 27

Garfield, James, 40
Geometry of pyramids, 4, 8–9, 25–28, 34–36; base 4, 26, 27, 35; height, 4, 8, 34, 35; perimeter, 8, 34; symbolism of, 25–28, 36; triangular sides, 26, 27, 28
Ghyka, Matila, 28
Gnostics, 27, 29
Goneid, Dr. Amr, 4
Great Pyramid at Giza, 4, 11–28, 29, 33–37, 77–78; builders of, 9, 40, 45, 78; casing stones, 29, 31, 34, 35; chambers, 21, 27, 33–34, 36, 49; computer study of, 2; engineering of, 7–9; functions of, 11, 15–16, 21–22; geometry, 4, 8, 9, 25–28, 34–35; Grand Gallery, 36, 39; measurements, 8–9, 31, 34–35; orientation of, 8, 45; passageways, 21, 36; siting of, 8, 31; size, 4, 7; stones of, 4, 7
Great Pyramid, The (Taylor), 35
Greaves, John, 31
Green, Dr. Elmer, 54

Green, Jules, 58–59

Hall, Manly P., 21–22, 27
Hermetic academies, 29
Herodotus, 29, 34
Hieroglyphics, 33
Himalayas, pyramid in, 45
History (Strabo), 30
Hittite civilization, 41

Initiation rites, 16, 21–22
Israel, lost tribes of, 35

Jung, Carl, 25

Ka (spiritual body), 22
Kabbalists, 29
Ki (force), 53
Kundalini (force), 53

Larcher, Hubert, 49, 50
Laser Stereo Conference System, 51
Life and Work at the Great Pyramid (Smyth), 35
Life force, 53
Liquids, experiments with, 55–57
Loehr, Franklin, 57–58

Mamun, Abdullah al, Caliph, 30–31
Mana (force), 53
Measuring systems, 35–36, 40
Menninger Foundation, 54
Menzies, Robert, 36
Mesopotamia, 11–12, 41
Metals, experiments with, 60
Mexico, pyramids of, 42, 45
Minoan civilization, 41–42
Moigno, Abbé F., 39
Mound cultures, 11, 12
Mummification, 16, 46, 49–50, 53
Mycenaean civilization, 41

Nanowave radiation, 52–53

(83)

ABOUT THE AUTHOR

A former Executive Director of the Parapsychology Foundation, and Research Officer of the Psychical Research Society, W. R. Akins has written numerous articles in the field. Currently he is working on a two-volume encyclopedia of psychic and occult studies. He is also the author of *ESP: Your Psychic Powers and How to Test Them* (A First Book), a book for young readers published by Franklin Watts.